THE INDIAN WAY

THE INDIAN WAY

Learning to Communicate
with Mother Earth

Gary McLain

Paintings by Gary McLain
Illustrations by Michael Taylor

John Muir Publications
Santa Fe, New Mexico

To Grandpa Iron

These full moon stories were told
to his kids, and their kids...

John Muir Publications, P.O. Box 613, Santa Fe, NM 87504

First edition. Sixth printing January 1993

Library of Congress Cataloging-in-Publication Data
McLain, Gary, 1941—
    The Indian way : learning to communicate with Mother Earth/ Gary McLain ; paintings by Gary
McLain ; illustrations by Michael Taylor. — 1st ed.
        p. cm.
    Includes bibliographical references.
    Summary: Describes how Native Americans viewed the environment, lived within it in harmony and
respect,
and how we today can learn from and practice Indian ways.
    ISBN 0-945465-73-4
    1. Indians of North America—Social life and customs—Juvenile literature. 2. Human ecology—North
America—Juvenile literature. [1. Indians of North America—Social life and customs. 2. Human ecology.
3. Ecology.] I. Title
E98.S7M27 1990
306'.089'97—dc20
                                                                                    90-36991
                                                                                    CIP
                                                                                    AC

CURR
E
98
.S7
m27
1993

Editor: Sheila Berg
Designer: Sally Blakemore
Typeface: Packard
Typesetter: Copygraphics, Santa Fe, New Mexico
Printer: Guynes Printing, Albuquerque, New Mexico

Distributed to the book trade by
W. W. Norton & Company, Inc.
New York, New York

Distributed to the education market by
The Wright Group
19201 120th Avenue NE
Bothell, WA 98011

CONTENTS

Preface vii

Introduction I

Full Moon Stories

First Moon—Mother Earth 5

Second Moon—The Food 9

Third Moon—The Home 13

Fourth Moon—Our Elders 17

Fifth Moon—Animals 21

Sixth Moon—Plants 25

Seventh Moon—The Sun 29

Eighth Moon—The Wind 33

Ninth Moon—Water 37

Tenth Moon—The Moon 41

Eleventh Moon—Sage Offerings 45

Twelfth Moon—The Four Directions 49

Thirteenth Moon—Art 53

Conclusion 59

Experiences

I Mother Earth 63 · 2 The Food 65 · 3 The Home 67

4 Our Elders 69 · 5 Animals 71 · 6 Plants 73 · 7 The Sun 75

8 The Wind 77 · 9 Water 79 · 10 The Moon 81

11 Sage Offerings 83 · 12 The Four Directions 85 · 13 Art 87

14 Games and Sports 89 · 15 Dances and Songs 91

16 Camping 93 · 17 The Sweat Lodge 95 · 18 The Vision Quest 97

19 The Sundance 99 · 20 Medicine Wheels 101

PREFACE

The Indian Way is about how Native Americans once looked at and lived within our environment. Many still follow this way today. It is a philosophy that has much to teach us.

All the stories in this book, about food, elders, the home, animals, art, and so forth, are closely related to each other, and all of these things make up the environment we live in. It is not good to live well in just one area of our lives and not others. All must receive equal attention.

While there are many different kinds of solutions offered to modern problems of pollution, waste, and abuse of the earth and sky, this way of seeing ourselves as just one part of—not better than—the landscape is a good beginning. If each of us starts from within ourself, we can reach out to the whole world and make it better for all earth's living things—people, animals, plants, water, and air.

Join with me to listen to Grandpa Iron's stories. Follow his wisdom.

INTRODUCTION

When I was a boy, I lived by the Wind River. My grandfather always told us kids a special story each time a full moon rose over the harsh landscape of the Wyoming plains.

Grandpa Iron is a Northern Arapahoe Medicine Man and the oldest elder in our Sundance Society. His stories were always closely related to the environment of the life of the Earth, our Mother. He never used the word environment in his life. Instead, he taught us how we, the two-legged ones, fit into the whole of all living things. He taught us the real happiness of being alive and how we are all responsible in our daily lives for all living things, our relatives.

Medicine People are teachers, healers, and spiritual leaders for all the people. They also know the history of the tribe. Stories were told and passed on to the next generation so that the people would always know their past. From these stories, Our People knew how to keep their good ways of life.

All us kids would sit in a circle around the old potbelly stove in Grandpa and Grandma Iron's log house and listen intently to the stories of wisdom the old man had to tell. He always smudged us with cedar smoke and said thank you to all living things before he began.

These are some of his full moon stories.

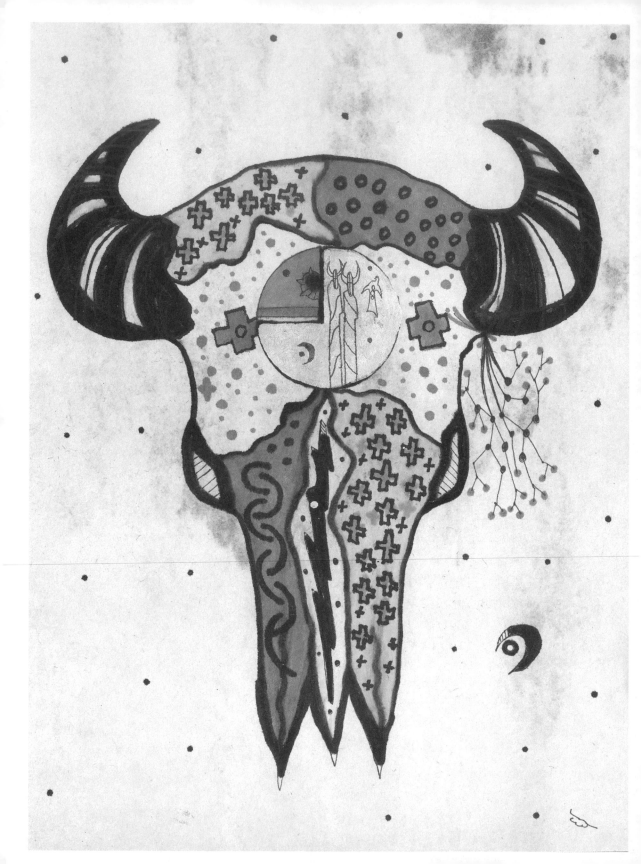

FULL MOON STORIES

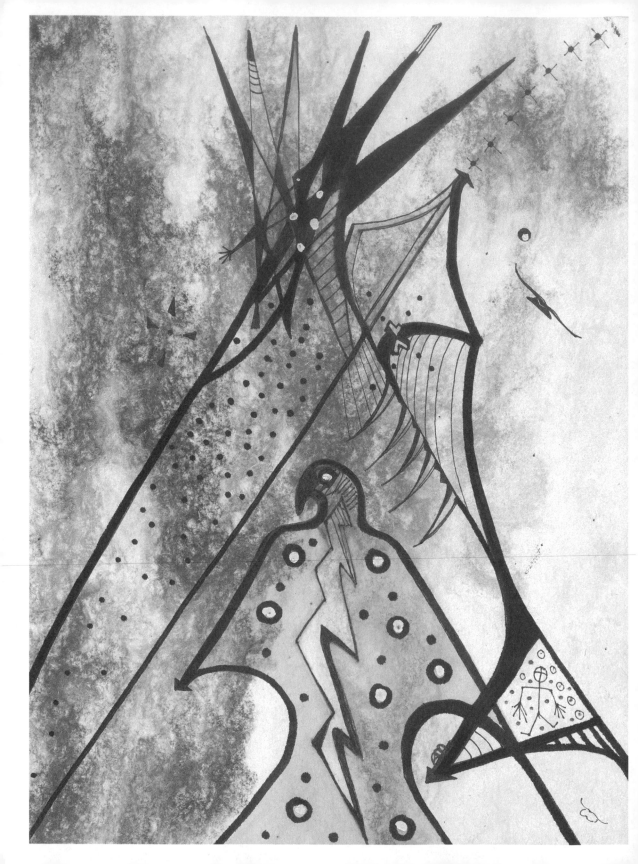

MOTHER EARTH

IN THE MOON WHEN THE SNOW BLOWS LIKE SPIRITS IN THE WIND, Grandpa Iron told us how Our People found the tipi and how it changed our lives.

Our People had always lived in caves and built their homes from bark and branches until one day some old men were sitting and watching children playing with cottonwood leaves. The children were stacking the leaves against each other in circles and using little sticks to keep them from falling down. So, the old men learned how to make tipis. We could now follow the buffalo and take our homes with us. The old people still say that we should always watch and listen to children.

Grandpa said that the tipi is a circle, as are all natural things in the world. The circle reminds us of our Mother Earth and of trees and plants. The circle stands for the sun, moon, and all round things in the Creation. The circle reminds us of the hoops of the tribes that lock together to form one great chain of circles.

Grandpa Iron would tell us to hold hands and form a circle. While the wind blew flakes of snow through the open cracks between the logs, we danced and sang the songs of the hoop Our People had known. Grandpa and Uncle Kail would laugh and tease us, telling us ''that's good, that's good,'' or ''lift your legs higher, lift your legs higher,'' while we danced on the worn board floor of the old log house.

Grandpa taught us that the circle means that all living things are related to each other on our Mother Earth. He told us we should respect everything that is alive. He taught us we should realize that our Mother, the Earth, is alive and that if we respect her, she will respect and take care of us.

He explained that our Mother Earth provides our food, clothing, water, and homes. We are each responsible for taking care of these things that she provides, and we are each responsible for teaching others to do the same. Take only what you need, and leave the land as you found it.

And then, while Grandma cooked our big meal of the day, we would run out and play barefooted in the snow until our feet were numb and we had to run back in by the stove to get warm. After our supper of skillet bread and deer meat, Grandma Iron would tuck us under the pile of quilts that were stacked on top of an iron frame bed. And we dreamed of circles and life.

And the Earth stayed young.

THE FOOD

WHEN THE MOON OF FROST SPARKLING IN THE SUN CAME, all us kids went to Grandpa Iron's house to hear another full moon story. He had said he was going to tell us a story about the food. But it was a hunting story, too, so we knew it was going to be a good one. A real good one.

We all sat down on the floor in a circle. Grandma gave us dry meat and water in a dipper from the white enamel bucket by the washstand. After we passed the dipper and everyone drank, Grandpa Iron smudged us with cedar smoke and began his full moon story.

He told about his grandson who was about 15 or 16 years old. He was given his first rifle since he was now a man. He went out hunting down by the river and got his first deer. It was good, very good. He went hunting the next day and he got another deer. It was good. But he continued to go hunting every day, day after day. And he always got a deer. They had so much meat they had to give it away. And then there was too much meat even to give away.

Pretty soon grandson got real sick and the family called Grandpa Iron for his help. Grandson had a high fever and could not move. Grandpa doctored him in the Indian medicine way and took out small deer hooves from his grandson's neck and back.

Grandson got well, but Grandpa Iron told him why he got sick. It is not good to take too much. It is not good to take more than you can use. You should always leave an offering of sage for thanks when you take another living thing for food. This is to thank their spirit for giving up their physical bodies for our food so we may live. Grandson hunted only when the family was in need, and he always remembered to offer sweet sage in thanks. It was good. It was very good.

When Grandpa finished his story, we went with Grandma to the big shed where she had bundles of sage stored. She gave us little bundles that we could always carry with us.

When we ate supper that night, Grandma told us that when we dropped our food it meant that the spirits of our ancestors are hungry.

As we slept, we dreamed of the spirits of the living things that give themselves to us for food. And we knew how important food is and how hard it can be to obtain in life.

The old log house smelled good with our little bundles of sweet sage stacked close to the door.

And the Earth stayed young.

THE HOME

IN THE MOON OF BUFFALO DROPPING THEIR CALVES, we had been at Grandpa's house for three days when we saw the full moon rising. Grandpa was sharpening knives on his stone grinder out by the tipi. It was close to evening and we saw the moon coming up above the plains. It was real red, like fire.

We gathered around him and asked him to tell us one of his full moon stories. It was getting cold, so he told us to go inside by the stove. He said he would join us as soon as he finished his work.

He came in with an armful of wood and laid it by the door. We sat as we were always taught, quietly waiting. We never had to be told more than once. Grandma taught us to never ask more than one time for anything we wanted.

Grandpa smudged us with the sweet-smelling cedar smoke and told us that this was going to be a medicine lesson.

He said everyone has the spirit of the Creation in their homes. Everything the home is made from and everything in it comes from the earth. This is a medicine power. The respect for this medicine is shown by honoring all those who live in the home. If elders come to visit or there are elders living in your home, you should never run in front of them or run in the house. You should not fight, jump, climb, play ball, or get loud. When you finish eating, you always thank the one who cooked the food and help put the food away.

Grandpa said that Grandma's sister, JéTon, would deal with kids that didn't behave, with her darning needles. He said if kids got too rowdy, the adults would tell them that Grandma JeTon was getting her sewing bag out—the one with the big darning needles in it.

Her ears had big holes in them from years of wearing heavy earrings, and the kids were scared of her. They thought she was going to pierce their ears and they would look like she did. The kids always sat very quiet and behaved when they were at her house.

Grandpa Iron said he didn't have any darning needles like Grandma JeTon, but she would always know if one of us kids didn't behave.

We always behaved.

We didn't want big holes in our ears.

And the Earth stayed young.

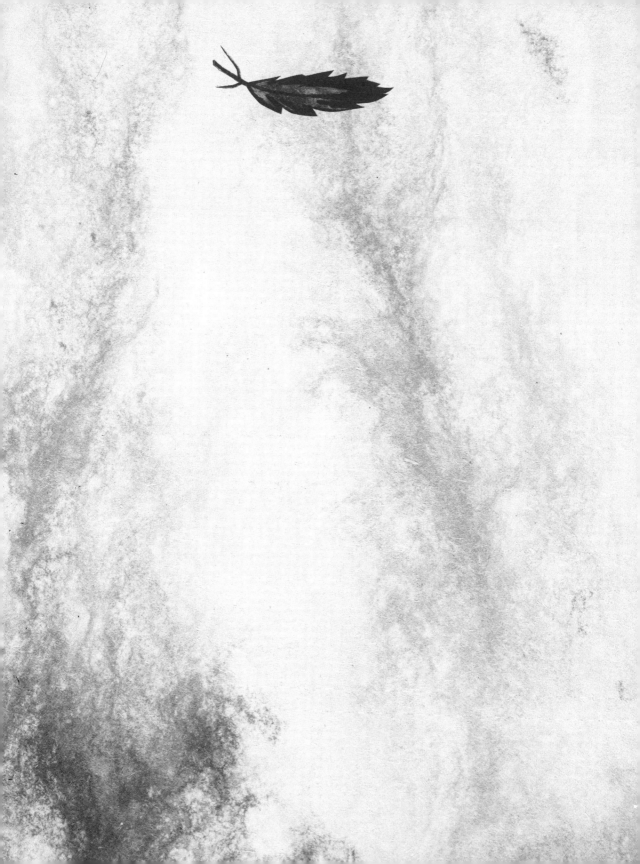

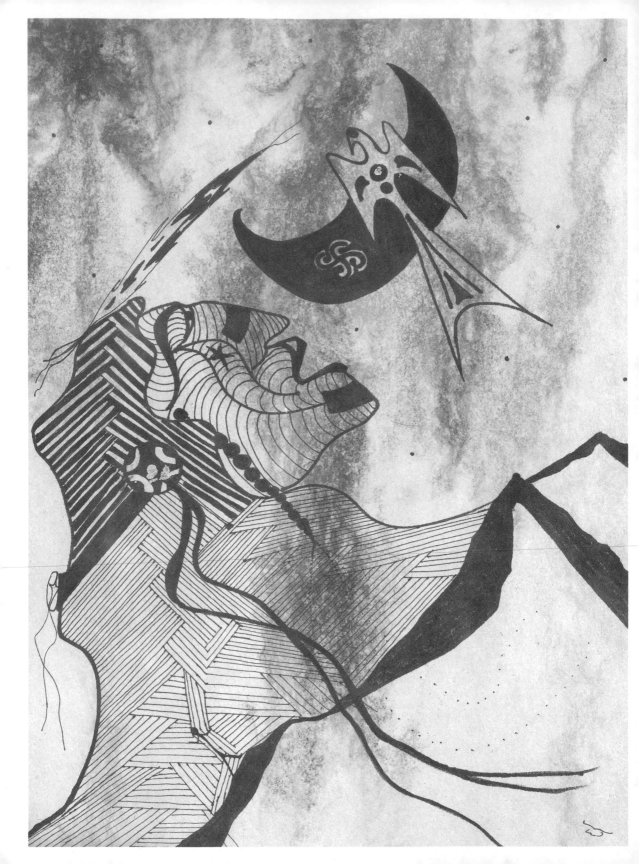

OUR ELDERS

WHEN THE MOON OF ICE BREAKING IN THE RIVER CAME, us kids were playing at the old powwow grounds. Uncle Kail stopped by in his old beat-up car to tell us that Grandpa Iron had a full moon story for us. We all piled in.

It was raining, and the car almost got stuck in the mud just before we got to Grandpa's house. The old logs of the house were rain soaked and gray. A trail of blue smoke rose straight up from the rusty stovepipe. His tipi looked lonely and alone with puddles of brown water surrounding it. The canvas was rain soaked, and water dripped from the streamers that hung straight down from the tips of the poles.

Inside the house it was warm by the stove and Grandma had ribs baking in the oven of the wood cookstove. The smell of wood burning combined with the odor of the deer meat cooking and the sweet smell of sage to make smells that didn't seem to like each other.

Grandpa gave us his blessing with the strong cedar smoke, and we sat down in a circle on the floor.

Grandpa sat down on the edge of his bed, and with his old ragged straw cowboy hat laying beside him, he told us a story about a three-legged one. (Sometimes when we get old or disabled, we need a cane to walk. Our People called these people the three-legged ones.)

Anyway, there was this old man who had hurt his leg one time when he was out hunting and ever since then he had to have a cane to walk. Well, as the years passed by he did okay, but he always had his wife and son to help him when he couldn't do something that was hard.

Then one time, when the camp was moving to follow the buffalo, the three-legged man's wife and son were both killed by a rock slide from a canyon wall while they were out looking for some medicine plants.

The old man was left alone with no one to help him in his life and with his third leg always with him. Life became very hard. There was no one to hunt food for him or to cook for him or to make his clothes.

Just when he thought he surely would die from starvation, another disaster came to the people. A man and woman from a tipi near the old man's own lodge were killed when they were caught in a flash flood while they were out catching fish from the nearby river. They left their only son alone and without any family to care for.

Well, you already know what happened. The young man needed a home and family to care for and the old three-legged man needed a son. They needed each other to live and to be happy. And they took each other for family, father and son. The young man hunted, and the old man cooked and kept the lodge. It was good. It was very good.

Grandpa Iron said we should always take care of our elders. They should eat first and be the first to get water when they're thirsty. Without our elders, we would not exist and all our future generations would not live. We must always respect our elders in their words and in their ways.

Grandma built up the fire in the potbelly stove and passed out fry bread for each of us, and water was passed around in the white enamel dipper.

We all thought that the world was a wonderful place to be. There in that old gray log house with the rain pouring down. In the middle of the reservation.

When Grandma tucked us under the pile of quilts that night, I remembered Grandpa's story and I knew I would always take care of them and I would always respect their ways.

And the Earth stayed young.

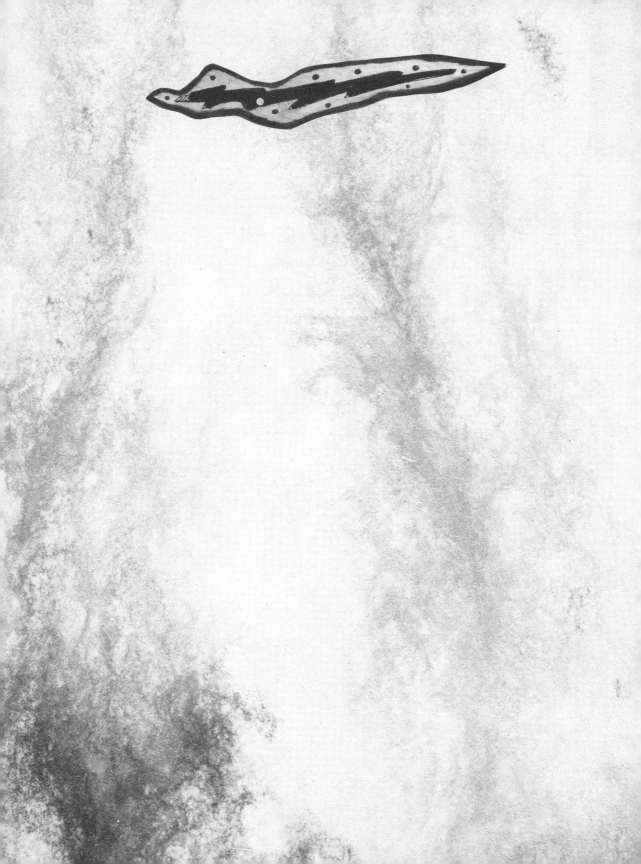

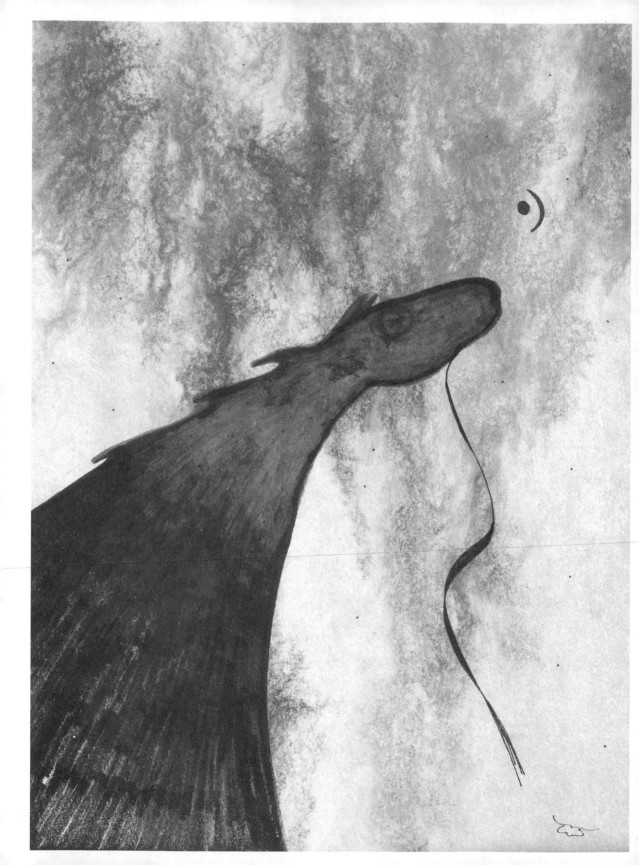

ANIMALS

IN THE MOON WHEN THE PONIES SHED THEIR SHAGGY HAIR, Grandpa and Grandma Iron had left us kids alone at the house while they went to town for groceries.

My sister, Betty, and I got hungry and decided to make bread. Since we watched Grandma make it every day, we thought it was easy.

Betty got the flour. I got the salt and the baking powder and the water. We started mixing it in a big metal pan. Then we remembered that Grandma put powdered milk in it, but we didn't know how to mix it.

There was a sudden knock on the door. We always locked ourselves in when our grandparents were gone. We peeked through the window and a white woman was standing there. I told Betty to ask the lady to mix the powdered milk for us. She said no, but I finally talked her into it. So she took the bowl of powdered milk to her.

The white woman was standing on the porch mixing the milk. I could smell the sweet odor of her perfume as I hid behind the door.

The lady left and Grandma and Grandpa came back. We never did get the bread in the oven. The kitchen part of the house was a mess. There was flour on the floor and dirty dishes all over. Then we noticed each other. We were a sight, all covered with flour and paste on our clothes and in our hair. Grandma said, ''What are you doing?'' Grandpa started laughing, but Grandma was real mad. We scurried to help her gather the dishes and Betty swept the floor.

Grandpa got all us kids together and burned cedar and smudged us off with the smoke.

He said that this full moon story was about little horses. They were real little horses, about the size of a fox. He said that when Our People lived free out on the plains, before the reservation, they followed the buffalo. Our People made their camps along rivers, close to water. The young boys used to walk away from the camp along the river and in the small hills. They used to see little horses and the boys had ropes made out of human hair. They would chase the little horses and try to rope them. But the little horses would run into holes in the riverbank. Sometimes they would wait for hours for them to come out, but they never did. The horses probably had other holes to get out of. Our People never did catch them.

Grandpa said that animals are our companions on Mother Earth. They help us in our work and some provide us with food. Others still live freely. All should have our respect and friendship.

When the story was over, I guess Grandma was still upset about the mess because she chased us all out to play.

My older brother Jimmy asked me to go hunting since the day was still young. It was the first time he had asked me to go and I was eager and happy that he wanted me to go along.

There was a big field about a mile and a half from Grandpa's house. We walked around the field on the edge. Jimmy had his .22 rifle and he said we were hunting pheasants for supper. He asked me to walk about ten feet in front of him, and he explained why. He said that the birds would hear my footsteps and vibrations and they would fly up so he could shoot them. I realized, years later, he had used me the same way others use a dog. But the pheasant sure tasted good. We left a sage offering after he shot the pheasants to thank their spirits.

That night, after supper, Grandpa sang to us some songs that honor animals and birds and all our friends that have four legs and fly and swim in the waters.

And the Earth stayed young.

PLANTS

IN THE MOON WHEN THE HOT WEATHER BEGINS, Grandpa hitched up the two big horses he kept to pull the wagon. He and Grandma were going to go out in the plains to pick up bones and iron that they could sell in town.

He told us kids that they would be back home in time for our full moon story and Grandma said we could stay with them for a while.

It seemed like the days turned into moons themselves, but late one evening, just before the full moon rose, they came by and picked us up. It was fun to ride in the wagon. We never missed our chance to sit on the back, swinging our legs and watching where we had been.

The old log house was cold and quiet until we got there. Before the full moon rose, Grandpa had the stove hot from a pine wood fire and Grandma had supper almost ready on the wood cookstove.

After Grandma fed us all an Indian stew made with potatoes, turnips, and fresh boiled meat, Grandpa divided up the rest of the fry bread among us kids and told us to sit in a circle on the floor.

He got out his cedar bag and sprinkled a few of the needles into a hot pan he kept on the wood stove for this purpose. After smoking us off with the cedar smoke and saying thanks to all living things, he began the full moon story.

A long time ago, when Our People still lived in wigwams made of bark and before we had the horse, Our People were food gatherers and farmers.

We lived toward that place where the sun rises and there are great waters that have no other side. We raised corn and some other vegetables for food, but we also gathered berries and roots that grew wild.

One time we had a hard year. There came a big cold wind from that direction where winter comes and a frost covered the land. It was late in the spring and it froze all the crops and all the wild foods that we lived on.

We had to send a party of Our People a long way to find food and to trade with other tribes for food. We barely had enough to live on until the next spring. This taught us to preserve food and store it for hard times.

Grandpa Iron said that all plants are our brothers and sisters. They talk to us, and if we listen we can hear them.

Plants not only provide us with food and medicine but they also provide wood for our homes and fuel for our fires. They hold the earth so that it cannot blow away or wash away. They provide the oxygen that we breathe. They are beautiful companions to us here on Mother Earth.

That night, I had dreams about the stories Grandpa told us about the plants. I dreamed of our ancestors and about the corn.

We still have some old kernels of corn in bundles that we saved from that time when we were farmers.

And the Earth stayed young.

THE SUN

IN THE MOON WHEN THE BUFFALO BELLOW, Uncle Kail brought my brother George and some of George's friends to Grandpa's house for a visit. George had been away for a long time, and we were all glad to see him.

In our traditional way, anyone that came to visit was always given food and coffee or water. It isn't polite to refuse anything that is good when it is offered to you.

So while everyone sat and ate, we went to swim in the river.

When we got back to the house, Grandpa told us that it was time to load the wagon with the tent and camp supplies. We knew it was Sundance time.

Everyone left to go to the Sundance grounds. When we got there, many people had already started to make camp. There was a lot of work to do and everyone helped set up our shadehouse and tent. Cooking pits were dug and wood was cut. Water was hauled in big cans. Tipis and tents and shade-houses began to fill the huge area.

Grandpa said he was going to be very busy with the Sundance so he was going to tell us our full moon story that night. The full moon wasn't due until several nights later, but this was the time of the first day of the Sun-dance, so our full moon story had to be early.

When evening came, Grandpa called all us kids to sit in the shade-house, and he smudged us off with cedar smoke before he began this full moon story.

Grandpa Iron said that we would hear the morning song coming from the Sundance lodge a few days from now. He said that the sun is the light of the universe and that the songs are for all life in the Creation. He told us that the sun brings the power of warmth and growth to all living things. Grandpa said that the sun is the medicine power in the Creation that stands for the Great Mystery, the Creator.

He said before the sun came, the universe was in darkness and cold. The spirits of all living things had no homes and were wandering through the blackness, searching for a place to become life. Then, one time when all the spirits came together and became one thought of hope, their wish for life exploded with light in the universe. The Earth, our Mother, was born, and the moon and all the planets and star nations were created.

The great power of the sun is the hope of love and goodness for all living things. Mother Earth gave herself to all life for the homes we needed. And the sun gave himself to all life for the light and warmth we needed.

Grandma fixed us plates of food from the big pot on the fire pit, and Grandpa Iron said a song to thank the food when we were all seated and ready to eat.

The sun set with an orange glow through gray clouds behind the Wind River Mountains and said good-bye to the evening star.

We laughed and giggled in our bedrolls on the floor of the shadehouse, the ground of Mother Earth, while the old people talked and drank coffee around the fire.

And I dreamed of the happy faces of Our People laughing in the sun.

And the Earth stayed young.

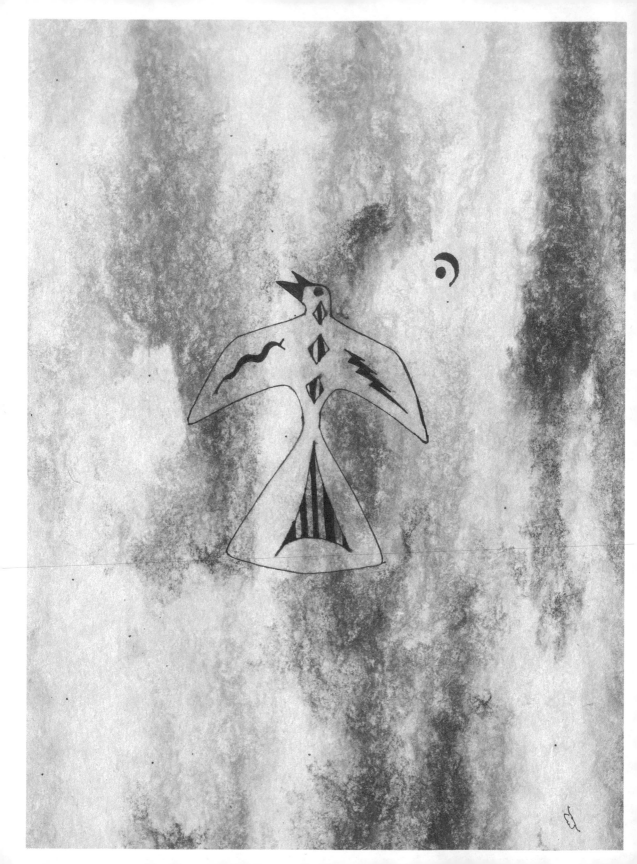

THE WIND

IN THE MOON WHEN THE CHOKECHERRIES BEGIN TO RIPEN, we were camped at the powwow grounds.

After the Sundance was over, we had moved to the powwow grounds for the big seven-day celebration that said we had had a good Sundance.

It was good to be outside and touching the Earth. Our People had now camped from full moon to full moon, and it seemed as if time was still. It was like it must have been when we still lived free on the plains and followed the buffalo.

Grandma sent us to pick berries down by the river. She gave us little buckets, and the older kids had kettles to fill. She told the oldest one of us to leave an offering before we started picking.

We were always glad when this time came because we knew that Grandma would fix us chokecherry pudding and fry bread. When we got down by the river and were picking, we saw a whirlwind and it looked like it was coming toward us. It looked real little until it got closer and then we knew it was really big and powerful. There were sticks and stones blowing around inside it and it was turning the color of the earth.

It did come straight toward us. We scattered, running to get out of its path. Everyone just dropped their pails and kettles of berries there in the bushes for the spirit of the wind.

We knew the whirlwind was a spirit, and we didn't want to be touched by it. We figured it must have been hungry, and it wanted our berries. So, we took our containers full of berries, leaving some behind.

When we got back to the camp, we told Grandpa what had happened.

He said that he already knew about it and that his full moon story that night would be about the wind.

When evening finally came and we had all stuffed ourselves on chokecherry pudding and fry bread, we helped Grandma with the dishes and cleaned up the shadehouse.

Grandpa sat by the little fire and got out his cedar bag so he could make a smudge to cedar us all off.

Then he began his full moon story about the wind.

A long time ago, a party of hunters was out looking for pronghorns (antelope), and since this was before the horse came to Our People, they were walking. The hunt had not been good. After they had been out away from their camp for several sunrises, they were tired and wanted to go back home. But they could not go back empty-handed.

Late one afternoon, when the sun was almost to say good-bye to the evening star, the leader of the group saw a cloud of dust rising up above the big flattop mountain Our People called Created by the Bear Butte. (Today it is called Devil's Tower. It is located in northwest Wyoming.)

The cloud of dust soon formed itself into a big whirlwind and then became even bigger. It was black and swirling; bigger and bigger. It began to gather great power, and pretty soon there were trees and even big stones spinning around with it and inside it.

It rose straight up and came straight toward them like a big monster rearing its head on the end of a long curving neck. It roared and made sounds like they had never heard before.

By this time, all the hunters had become afraid and wondered which way to run. Their leader had to make a decision fast. So, he yelled over the big wind noise for them to follow him.

He ran straight toward the big wind spirit; all the hunters fell in behind and ran hunched over against the strong wind. Just when it seemed that the big wind would swallow them up, a hole appeared at the edge of a small gully. A big flat rock formed the roof of the small cave, and there was just enough room for the hunters to all get inside. The monster wind went right over them, roaring and throwing dust and stones into their little hole. And then it was gone.

The hunters were so scared and so tired that they spent the night in the small gully where the whirlwind had chased them.

The next morning, as they awoke with the new sun, they were surprised and happy to see a herd of antelope all around their cave. They went back to their camp with lots of good meat. All the people ate and were happy. The big wind had brought food so the people might live, and the big wind had taught Our People how to hunt the antelope from holes in the ground.

Grandpa said that the wind is related to the Thunder Beings and that the power of rain and thunder and lightning is good for all living things. He said that the wind is the breath of our Mother, the Earth, and to breathe the wind is taking and sharing her power within yourself.

Grandma told us to get our bedrolls out and lay them on the ground. It was time to go to bed. Tomorrow we all had to go back to our own homes. Grandma and Grandpa were breaking camp and going back to their house. The summer Sundance and powwow were over until next year.

And the Earth stayed young.

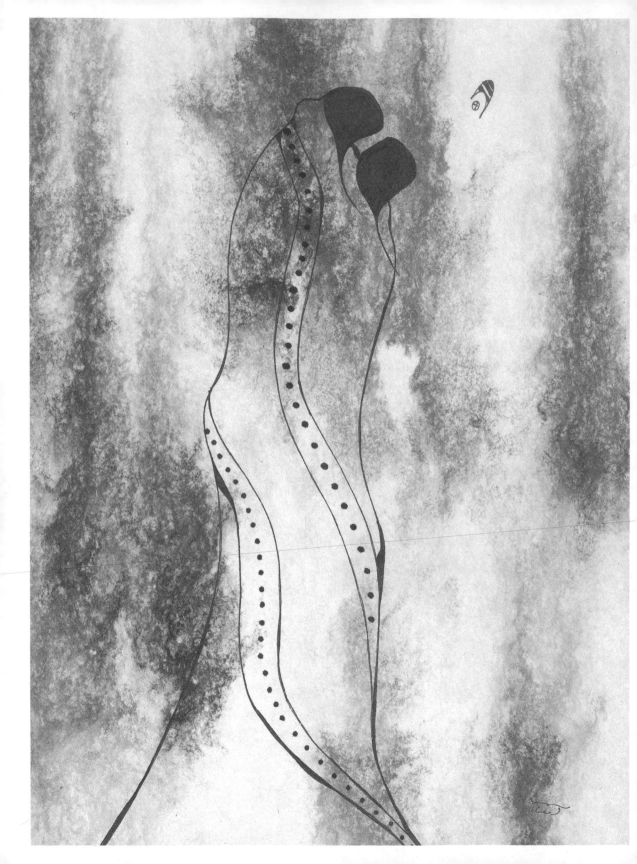

WATER

WHEN THE MOON OF GEESE SHEDDING THEIR FEATHERS CAME, us kids went up to Grandpa's house to see if there was going to be a full moon story. We knew summer was almost over, and we also knew that school would soon be starting. It seemed as though the summer had flown away like Grandpa's story of the big whirlwind. It was here and then it was gone.

The days were still warm. We spent a lot of time swimming in the river and playing like we were still living wild and free. We didn't know exactly how life had been when Our People lived in tipis and followed the buffalo, but I guess Grandpa had given us enough information in his stories to give us a pretty good idea.

Anyway, Grandpa was out by the old makeshift corral where he kept the big workhorses that pulled his wagon. The horses nickered a greeting to us as we walked up, and Grandpa laughed and told us that they were happy to see us, as he was.

After he finished feeding and watering the horses, we all walked back to the house with him. Inside, we found Grandma patching a quilt. She finished her task and then told us to sit down while she fixed something for everyone to eat. While she cooked, she got after us for swimming so much. She said we were going to get scales like the fishes. Grandpa always laughed when she got after us.

After we ate a good supper of Indian stew and cornbread and beans, we sat down in a circle on the floor and waited for Grandpa to come in and tell us our full moon story. He arrived carrying the pan with the smouldering cedar in it. The smoke trailed up and back over his shoulder as he walked.

After he smudged us off with the cedar smoke, he took down his hat from the wall and laid it on the bed. Then he sat down and began the full moon story about water.

One time there was a young man named Bluebird who liked to go over and visit with other boys in another camp that was close to Our People's camp. The other camp was a band of Shyelas (Cheyennes), and there was a pretty girl there called Little Star who was a sister to the boys. She was very pretty, and our young man was really going over to see her. He was just pretending to go see her brothers.

Anyway, one time when Bluebird was over there visiting, and pretending, a big storm came up from the direction where the sun goes down. The Thunder Beings were big and black, and there was thunder and lightning and plenty of rain. Good rain to give life to all the things that grow and make the grass deep and green for the buffalo and for our horses.

Bluebird had his three horses tied to a tether rope between two trees. When one of the big clouds spoke loud with thunder and lightning, two of the horses broke away. Bluebird ran back to his camp when the storm came. He got to his tipi just as the two horses broke away, jumping and snorting and blowing wind. They ran right through the Shyela camp and up the river toward the storm and in the rain.

Well, Bluebird knew he had to catch them right away. They were fine ponies, and anyone would have been glad to catch them and claim them for their own. He mounted the only pony left and made chase after them. He caught one of the ponies right away by the river.

Little Star, the girl Bluebird liked so much, was right there where he caught the first pony. She had just drawn some water from the river and was standing in the willows watching him.

Bluebird wanted to stop and talk to her because it was the first time they had ever been alone. But the other pony was still gone, and he had to catch it. So he handed the rope from the first pony he had caught to Little Star and asked her to hold it until he got back.

Away up the river he went, chasing the last pony. It was a long time before he caught him, and the sun was going down and saying hello to the evening star before he started back to the willows where Little Star had been. He thought she would be gone since it had been so long. He thought she would just tie up the pony to a willow and go on home.

When Bluebird rode around the bend in the river into the willow thicket, Little Star was standing in the same spot still holding the rope.

The Thunder Beings had been good to Bluebird this day.

Grandpa laughed and we all laughed. It had been a good story and everyone liked it.

Grandpa said that the water is the blood of our Mother Earth. The rain washes the air and the streams wash the Earth. Without water nothing could grow and without water we are nothing. It is good to say thank you for all the clean water that the Creation has provided for us for no life can exist without water.

Grandma passed out leftover cornbread and dippers of clean cold water to all us kids. It sure tasted good.

And the Earth stayed young.

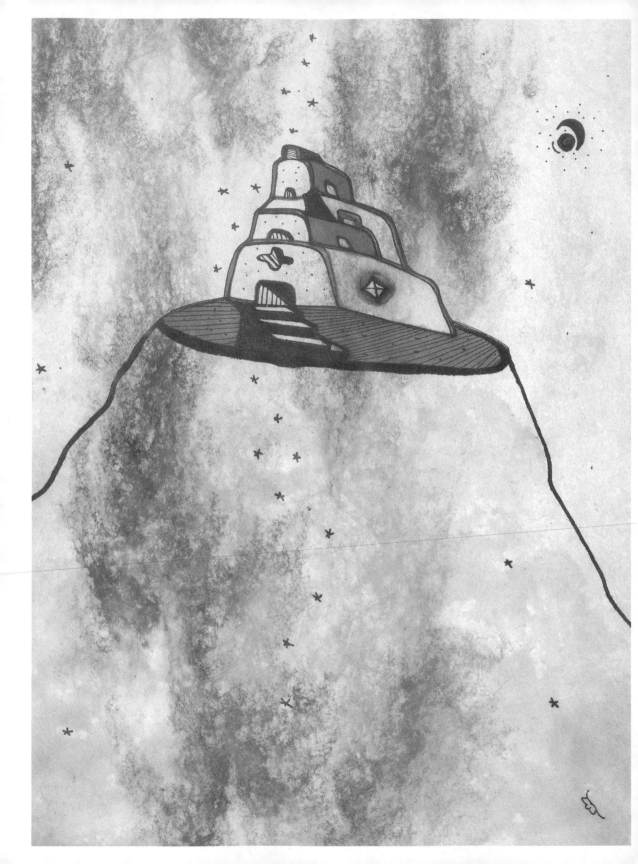

THE MOON

IN THE MOON OF DRYING GRASS, the full moon rose like a fire over the plains. Smoke from the cooking fire laid in the low areas along the Wind River and looked like spirits running through the trees in the bright moonlight.

All us kids had been playing in the woods, and the smoke spirits chased us back to Grandpa's house.

Grandpa and Grandma were out behind the house where Grandma had been cutting long strips of deer meat to dry in the hot September sun. Their boys were good hunters and always brought lots of meat to last through the long winter.

Grandpa laughed when we told him about the smoke spirits. But Grandma scolded him and told him to get back to work since it was getting late. He laughed again. He always laughed when she scolded him.

Grandma told us to go inside and help Grandpa build a fire in the cookstove while she covered the drying meat strips with cheesecloth to keep the magpies from stealing too much of it the next morning. The magpies always came early in the morning. I guess they didn't ever learn that Grandma and Grandpa got up with the sun.

Grandma cooked us a good supper of fresh deer meat, fried until it was crispy on the edges. Just the way I liked it the best. And we had skillet bread and gravy and lots of good cold water.

After supper we helped with the dishes and cleaned up the kitchen part of the house. Grandpa had the coal oil lamp lit and his hat was laying on the bed.

We knew it was almost time for our full moon story.

Grandpa said that the moon was clear up above the rim of the world and bright in the clear sky. He called us all to look at her face through the window. Then he smoked us off, and we sat on the floor. He began our full moon story about the moon.

One time, when Our People lived out on the plains, two young girls who were sisters were standing outside their parents' tipi in the moonlight. They were looking up at all the star nations in that great strip of stars across the sky. They saw the group of stars we called Carrier (the Big Dipper), and they wondered if people lived there, too. They looked at the moon, and they wondered if people lived there. And they wondered why the moon changes shapes and comes and goes instead of staying round like the sun does. They were just full of wonder.

It was fun to look at the star nations in the bright moonlight and wonder about all the mystery of the Creation.

A falling star streaked across the sky and fell behind the trees across the river from the camp. Another falling star streaked across the sky and fell behind the trees.

The wondering girls just wondered more. Just then, two glows appeared in the woods over there by the river, and through the smoke from the camp the glowing shapes looked like two young men. They were beautiful young men. At least the two young girls thought so.

The girls were afraid and wanted to run inside. But then the young smoke spirit men from the stars came close and spoke to them. And they were so handsome and so gentle that the girls were no longer afraid.

The star men told the girls that they had come to tell them about the star nations and the moon. They said they had heard the girls wondering and had come to tell them about all the wonderful places in the universe.

The star men said there was a village above a great flat plain in the stars. On this plain the people lived in peace and harmony with each other and all living things. There was plenty of food and clean water, and no one got gray hairs and uprooted teeth. There were no three-leggeds, and everyone stayed young. The star men said that the moon shone on their nation like the sun shone on ours and that the moon always stayed round when you saw it from the other side. It was good. It was very good.

The star men gave the girls gifts they had brought from their star nation. One of the gifts was the gift of knowledge. If we wonder often, the gift of knowledge will come often to us, too.

The star men went back to their homes. And the young girls dreamed of a beautiful village on the top of a big hill in the stars.

Grandpa said that when we see the moon change, and come and go again, that it is like life. With change there is growth, and everything lives and dies.

Grandma put us to bed under the quilts on the iron frame bed. I dreamed of the star men and that I was flying with them to their star nation in the sky.

And the Earth stayed young.

SAGE OFFERINGS

WHEN THE MOON OF FALLING LEAVES CAME WITH THE FIRST FROSTS OF WINTER, Grandpa and Grandma took us with them to their neighbors' house. The neighbors were old people, and they had asked Grandpa to help butcher a cow. Grandma was there to help cut up the meat and make some into dried strips to store for the winter.

Grandpa offered sage to the spirit of the cow that was giving up its life so we could live.

While our elders did the butchering, us kids played like we were great hunters and the tribe was celebrating our coming home, with lots of food for the people.

After we all got back home that evening, our sister, the full moon, rose above the plains and turned into a silver globe in the dark blue sky.

After supper, Grandpa showed us how to cedar ourselves. He said that the smoke from the cedar purifies our minds and bodies. It is good to burn a few small cedar needles and allow the smoke to clean our bodies. Then he said a blessing for the day and for all the good things that the Creation provides for us.

Then, after were were seated, he started telling the full moon story.

He said that sage grows all around our Mother Earth. Grandpa told us that when the star men brought the gift of knowledge from the heavens, they also brought the sage. It represents the powers of the Creation, and it means that our minds and our hearts are close to the Creator. The powers in the sage represent the things of the universe, the stars, and the planets, which are very mysterious.

Grandpa said that when we offer sage to other living things, we are offering a gift that stands for our respect for all life. When we show our respect for other living things, they respond with respect for us.

Grandma gave each of us little buckskin bags that she had sewed for us to keep our sage in. They were sewn with bird and porcupine quills dyed in the colors of the four directions. They were beautiful gifts.

We fell asleep while Grandpa sang the evening star song.

And the Earth stayed young.

THE FOUR DIRECTIONS

IN THE MOON WHEN THE RIVERS START TO FREEZE, we started walking to Grandpa's house as the sun was saying hello to the evening star.

When we were about halfway there, we heard something mocking us. We would laugh and talk, and then it would laugh and talk. We got scared and started running. When we reached Grandpa's house, we told him what had happened. He laughed a little and told us what it was.

It was an owl, he said. The spirits of our ancestors sometimes live in owls. He was mocking us because we were too loud and getting silly and not thinking about what we were doing.

Grandma said she would feed the spirits of our ancestors to apologize for our disrespect. Before supper, she left morsels of food outside the door.

After our meal was over, Grandpa sat us down and cedared us all off with the sweet-smelling smoke. After laying his cowboy hat on the bed, he stood in the center of the circle we formed around him on the floor.

He faced the west, and he told us that it is the direction where the Thunder Beings live. Its color is blue gray like the storm clouds. It has the power of rain that gives life. He said that the lightning and the bow stand for the powers to kill so we may have food, and the wooden cup stands for the rain.

He faced the north, and he said that it is the direction where the Great White Giant lives. Its color is white like the snows that come on winds of cleansing and healing in the winter. The white goose feather stands for the clean snow, and the white medicine herb from the north stands for the healing power of that direction.

Grandpa faced the east and talked about the peace and harmony found in that direction. He said that our sacred pipe stands for peace and that the morning star stands for the wisdom that peace and harmony bring to our lives. Its color is red like the sunrise.

He faced the south and he told us that its color is yellow like the summer sun. The six sacred branches stand for warmth. The little hoop stands for the circles of Our People that grow with the life that the sun gives.

Grandpa walked from the south direction toward the north and he said that it was like a road, a road of spirit, and that it is the good red road.

He walked from the east direction toward the west, and he told us that it was also a road, the black road of life. He said it was a road of trouble and need, but if we walked both roads in balance we will find the center where the roads cross. At the center grows the tree of life. If we water the tree, it will grow and fill with leaves and blooms and singing birds. He said that the center of the roads is found in our hearts and that all the good things from the four directions would come into our lives if we always remembered to water the tree.

Before I fell asleep that night, I heard an owl calling out to another owl in the woods by the river. He was telling the tale of how he frightened us and how he had taught us to show respect for all our relatives in the universe.

The colors of the four directions were in my dreams, and I remember dreaming of a small tree pushing its way up through dry, cracked earth.

And the Earth stayed young.

ART

WHEN THE MOON OF POPPING TREES CAME TO WIND RIVER, us kids were sliding on the ice across the shallow ponds behind the house.

The trees by the river made snapping sounds from the cold as the wind blew. Each time we got cold and numb from the cold wind, we ran into the house and warmed up by the potbelly wood stove.

Grandma started cooking supper early in the afternoon, and Grandpa brought in armsful of split cottonwood to keep us warm through the night.

Somewhere, from a long way off, the sound of horses nickering sounded like spirits crying in the wind. And the sounds of the trees popping combined with the whistles of the wind coming through the cracks in the house and the horses nickering to make Indian music.

Grandpa started to sing Sundance songs when he had the stove hot. We sat around by him and remembered when the sun was warm and we had had such fun last summer. The time we spent camping and swimming and being outside for weeks seemed a long time ago.

Grandma gave us each little jobs to do on these long, cold winter days. And sometimes we would make beaded earrings or our own toys to keep ourselves occupied when it was too cold to be outside.

Art is to Our People a part of our lives and not something that is separated from day-to-day life. Making beaded earrings, beaded belts, or hair ties or braiding horsehair into hat bands or bridles for our horses is, to us, a way to make things we need in a beautiful way.

The same is true of our games and sports and our dances and songs.

Everything we do seems to be so natural and in tune with all of life. I guess this is because everything in our ''arts'' relates to some part of our own life as well as to the lives of all living things, our relatives.

Anyway, after we had all eaten supper, Grandpa heated up the old enameled pan he burned cedar in and smoked us off. The full moon story, he said, would be about how Our People learned to live in tipis through the long, cold winters on the plains.

We used to make a pile of wood by each tipi almost as big as the tipi itself to last all winter. The cover of the lodge was left up off the ground and the liner inside was pulled down tight to the ground so the tipi became its own chimney. The fresh air from outside would go up between the cover and the liner and carry the smoke on out from the fire on the ground in the center of the lodge. This way only a small fire would heat the tipi.

Buffalo robes were stacked in big piles for beds, and when it came time to go to bed, you had to only burrow as deep as necessary to keep warm. Real cold nights meant that a lot of robes were laid over the top.

The days were spent repairing and making new moccasins, clothing from buckskins, tipis from buffalo hides, drums, whistles, flutes, and hunting equipment such as bows, arrows, and lances. When these things were made, there was time to decorate and do artwork on them with quills, paints made from plant and earth dyes mixed with buffalo tallow, feathers, and stones. Sinew, the stringy part of the buffalo's back, was used for sewing thread, and needles were made of bone splinters.

The long, cold days gave the people time to sing songs and dance. They would gather outside around a community fire for dance celebrations when the days were not too cold or when it wasn't storming. Over the passage of years and years, all the art forms of Our People became refined from pride into beauty. Our art is filled with symbols that stand for all the life forms we know about, and many symbols defined things we know little about but that are full of mystery.

Stories and the history of the tribe were painted on buffalo robes and passed down to the younger generations. They were usually kept by one family. These were called winter count robes. Only those people who had been taught the importance of the robes could keep them.

Our songs are usually chants, but often they contain words of our language. The drumbeat is the heartbeat of our Mother Earth. The combination of the drumbeat and the chants makes songs that define many things. There are happy songs for celebrations and sad songs for bad times. There are songs for babies and little children. And there are songs for honor and even weddings. Songs are sung for horses and other animals, even for the plants.

When the weather became warmer, with the coming of spring, Our People had time for games and sports. The children played stickball, a game played with sticks and a leather ball on the ground. It's almost like hockey is played today.

Using forked sticks, the boys played a game of slinging mudballs at each other. This taught them to endure pain. Boys threw arrows at rolling medicine wheel hoops made from willow branches and strips of soft bark. They tested their riding skills by pulling each other off their ponies, and they learned how to fall without being hurt. And, they learned how to lose without anger but still take pride in winning.

The young girls would have little tipis for playhouses, and they held contests to see who would put up their tipi fastest.

The older men had a game they called stickball, too. A hard leather ball was thrown with a stick that had a sinew webbing on the end. It was cupped to hold the ball until it was slung. You could even catch the ball with it. Teams were chosen. They played against each other until one side had moved the ball through the other team. It could be a very rough game.

So, the culture of Our People was good. It was very good. We cared for each other, and we cared for all living things. Our ways showed that caring in everything we did. Even in our art, sports, and songs. We danced with the happiness of our good life. Life could be hard and often was, but the

Earth stayed clean and green and the sky stayed blue. The water ran clean and gave life to all things.

Grandpa said to always remember these things and to teach our own children.

Grandma tucked us into bed, and I fell asleep as Grandpa sang the song of our Mother Earth.

And the Earth stayed young.

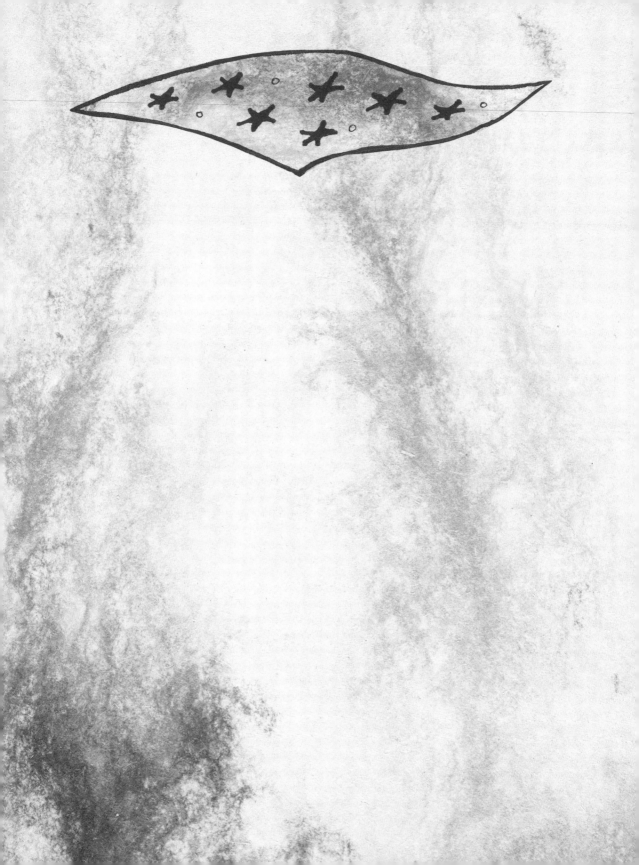

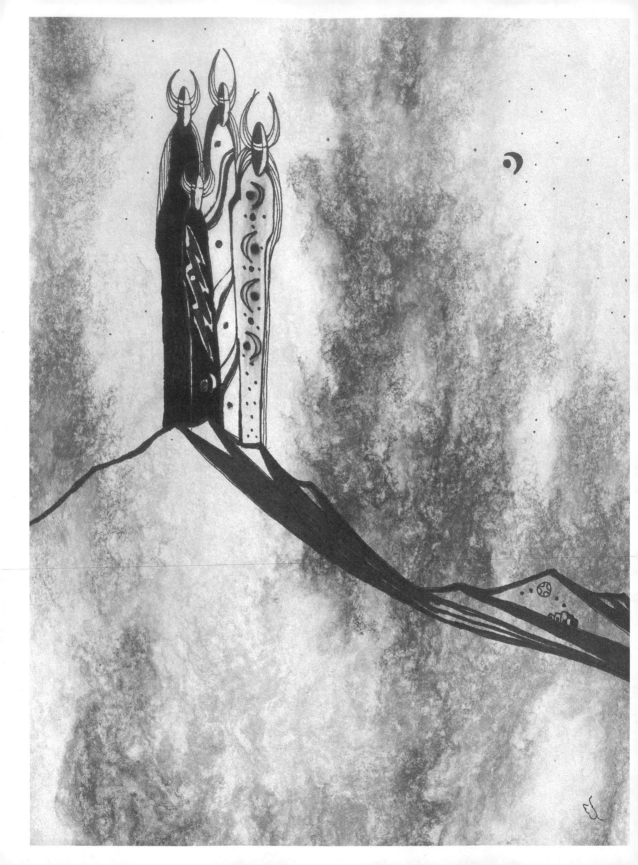

CONCLUSION

As the years passed by and I became a man, I realized the wisdom of my Grandfather's words. Words have great power. They carry the knowledge of our ancestors to our children.

As I look at the world now, I know what he meant by his stories. In our world now, I see the pollution in the air; rivers poisoned with chemical waste; animals, trees, and plants dying from acid rain; and oceans thick with our garbage and oil spills. All these things and more happen out of our disrespect for our Mother Earth and out of our disrespect for each other.

Greed has blinded us so we no longer see with our hearts. We no longer hear the animals and plants talking to us. Our world is filled with the sounds of machines. We do not take time to communicate with nature.

You can change the conditions that caused our Mother Earth to become ill. We do not have to go back and live the old way. We only need to use all those ways of life that did not harm the Earth. We can use all those good things that our technology provides and all those good ways of the past together.

If all the people of our Mother Earth make this their goal, the Earth's wounds will heal and she will provide a good safe home for us. Think of the whole earth as our home, not just one little part of it. When something happens that hurts the environment anywhere on our Mother Earth, it hurts us and our immediate environment also.

Sing the songs of our Mother Earth, and she will be young again.

EXPERIENCES

I

MOTHER EARTH

In the Moon of Snow Blowing Spirits in the Wind (January), Grandpa Iron taught us the ways of living with respect for our Mother Earth.

Run and play and sit down on the earth. Feel her soil with your hands. Walk barefooted and feel her between your toes. She is here for you and will never abandon you if you care for her.

Make up a song to sing for Mother Earth.

Sit cross-legged on the ground, in a circle with the other kids, and tell the story of how the tipi came to Our People and how it changed our lives.

Sleep and dream of circles and life.

It is good.

2

THE FOOD

In the Moon of Frost Shining in the Sun (February), Grandpa Iron told us how important the food is. It is first before all things and as important to us as life.

Before eating, always take a little time to thank the food. And never take more than you need so there will be no waste.

It is fun to go out in the woods and pick berries and thank the plants for their gifts. Go with your parents or an adult so you will know if what you want to pick is good to eat.

Offer the plants a little sweet sage for giving themselves to you.

Even when you eat out at a restaurant, you should remember the spirits of the living things that gave themselves to you for food. Hamburgers and french fries were living things, too.

It is good.

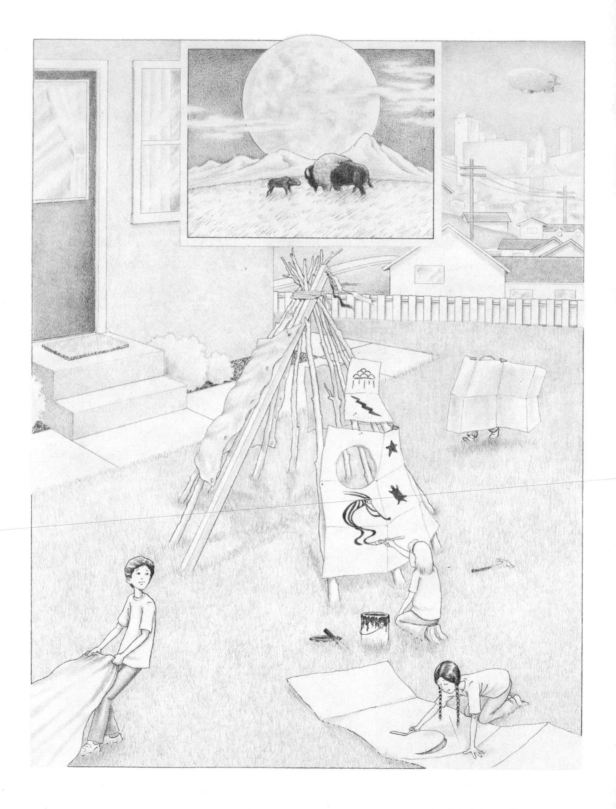

3

THE HOME

In the Moon When the Buffalo Calves Are Born (March), Grandpa taught us we should respect our homes.

Help your elders clean the house. Help with the dishes and clean your room. It's fun to have a nice, clean room and house to live in. This will bring you honor and respect from your parents and everyone in your home.

Set up a small tipi, playhouse, or treehouse out in the yard or in a place away from bothering your parents. Pretend like you are grown up and you are the parents. Ask your "children" to behave like they should in your home. If they don't, their ears could look like Grandma JeTon's!

It is good.

4

OUR ELDERS

In the Moon of Ice Breaking in the River (April), Grandpa Iron taught us to respect our elders.

You can do something special for an elder in your own home. Or you can do something special for your parents. Take them some flowers or draw a picture for them. Ask them what they would like you to do for them.

Maybe there is a home nearby where old people live. Take them a gift, or flowers, or a drawing you have done. Ask them if there is anything they need that you can do.

Ask your teacher in school to arrange for your class to visit a home for the elderly. Their day will be brighter for your visit to them with the little gifts you bring.

It is good.

5

ANIMALS

In the Moon When the Ponies Shed Their Shaggy Hair (May), Grandpa sang us songs that show respect for all our animal brothers and sisters.

You can show your own caring for them also. Take special care of your pets, and remember how lonely our Mother Earth would be without all the animal kingdom.

Speak out against those people who kill animals for sport or for money. We should only kill animals for food and then only take what we need.

Tell other kids what you have learned about our animal brothers and sisters.

With our love and respect, all animals can share our beautiful Mother Earth with us.

It is good.

6

PLANTS

In the Moon When the Hot Weather Begins (June), Grandpa Iron told us stories about plants.

You can raise plants or make a little garden where you live.

If you live in an apartment in the city, you can grow small plants in pots or a window box.

If you live in the country, you can plant a garden in the yard or in the corner of a field.

Go to the park and the zoo. Listen to the plants talking.

You can walk in the woods and listen to the trees talking to you.

Always go with your parents or an adult; never go alone until you are an adult.

It is good.

7

THE SUN

In the Moon When the Buffalo Bellow (July), Grandpa Iron told us about the sun and what it means in our lives.

The sun is powerful. It provides us with the clean power of electricity and energy. It purifies our air and water.

You can get up and greet the sun each morning. Stand facing the sun and raise your arms to the moment when he breaks above the horizon.

Say thank you for all the powers of warmth and light that the sun provides for us. Remember that the light and warmth is for all living things, all our relatives, and yourself.

It is good.

8

THE WIND

In the Moon When the Chokecherries Begin to Ripen (late July), Grandpa Iron told us about the wind and that it is related to the Thunder Beings.

The wind carries the clouds that bring the rain, and it cools the air. The wind provides good, clean energy.

You can enjoy the wind.

Make or buy a kite and fly it on the wind. Paint the designs of the sun and universe on it.

Enjoy walking with the wind on a day when it is really blowing. Lean into it, and then let it push you along.

Be as a brother or sister to the wind. Breathe the breath of our Mother Earth.

Listen to the wind in the trees and wonder what it is saying to you. You can hear it talking.

Is it telling Grandpa's story of the time the wind saved the people?

It is good.

9

WATER

In the Moon of Geese Shedding Their Feathers (August), Grandpa told us the story of Bluebird and how the Thunder Beings had been good to him.

Think of all the ways you use water in your life.

Think of all the life that lives in the waters and study about that life in your library.

When you drink water, take a little time to give thanks for the good things it does for us. Without clean water, we will not live.

Think of all the ways the Thunder Beings are good to you.

Make a list of the ways you use water every day. Make a list of how much water you use and ways to save water. It is not good to waste anything.

It is good.

10

THE MOON

In the Moon of the Drying Grass (September), Grandpa Iron told us the story of the two sisters who liked to wonder about the mysteries of the universe.

Read more about the moon in your library.

Draw the phases of the moon, and learn the names of the different moons.

Look on your calendar. When the moon changes, go outside and look at the moon in the sky. Is it the same shape as the one on your calendar?

Color the different shapes of the moon and cut them out with scissors. Hang them on the wall of your room.

Do you wonder about the moon and the star nations in the universe?

It is good.

SAGE OFFERINGS

In the Moon of Falling Leaves (October), Grandpa told us about the gift of sage from the star men. He told us that if we are good to living things, they will be good to us. He told us that all living things should have our respect.

You can use sage as an offering to give thanks for food as you gather it.

Make a small cloth or leather bag with a drawstring top to keep your medicine herbs in. Decorate it with designs of birds or animals. Fabric paints are available at dry goods stores.

Sage is available at many Indian shops if you are unable to pick it where you live.

It is good.

12

THE FOUR DIRECTIONS

In the Moon When the Rivers Start to Freeze (November), Grandpa told us about the four directions and the tree of life.

Draw a medicine wheel with the four directions. Color them like Grandpa said. Make the "road" from south to north red and the "road" from east to west black. Draw a tree where the roads cross. Make the tree bloom and fill with singing birds.

Cut it out and hang it on your wall, or give it to someone as a gift. Explain what the colors and the roads and the tree represent.

It is good.

13

ART

In the Moon of Popping Trees (December), Grandpa Iron told us how Our People use art in our lives. It is our expression of the beauty of the world. Our Mother Earth is the gallery that shows her beautiful art.

You can go to a hobby shop and buy a small beading loom and supplies. It will also have a book that shows Indian designs and tells how to do beadwork.

You can paint Indian designs, on your own, on cloth and leather with fabric paint available at hobby shops.

Ask your teacher if your class can do a project on Indian art in school. It is good.

14

GAMES AND SPORTS

In the Moon of Popping Trees (December), Grandpa told us some of the games and sports of Our People and about how besides being fun, they often prepared us for life.

Another game that is fun is called the handgame, a guessing game. It is for two players or more.

Cut four sticks about the size of a pencil. Or use four pencils of different colors. Place these sticks in the center between the players. Cut two short sticks small enough to hide in each hand. Put a mark on or color one of the short sticks.

Take turns holding the short sticks, one in each hand, while the person or persons on the other side guess which hand has the marked stick. If they guess correct, they win one of the long sticks. If they are wrong, the short sticks pass to the other player and he gets a chance to guess. The player who ends up with all the long sticks is the winner.

It is good.

15

DANCES AND SONGS

In the Moon of Popping Trees (December), Grandpa told us about the dances and songs of Our People.

You can make a drum from an oatmeal box with rubber stretched across the open ends. Make a drumstick with a pencil, and pad one end with cloth or leather.

You and other kids can dance sideways in a circle (the Round Dance) while one beats the drum in a slow, steady beat. Don't beat the drum like you hear it in the movies. It is supposed to be slow and steady and soft.

Move your feet sideways one at a time with each beat of the drum.

Think about how the drumbeat is the heartbeat of our Mother Earth. Indian tapes of songs are available at Indian shops, and some libraries will loan tapes to you.

It is good.

16

CAMPING

In Grandpa's stories, we learned that it is fun to go camping. We camped for a whole month each summer during the Sundance and the powwow after it, and we had great fun.

When you go camping, with your parents or other adults, there are rules to follow just like in all of life.

Keep your camp clean, and don't waste anything.

Don't litter the earth, and don't litter the lakes, rivers, and streams.

Put fires out with water and dirt.

Don't cut live trees, and don't destroy any plants.

Give the animals all the respect that you give to each other.

Tell each other the full moon stories as you are sitting around the campfire in the evening.

It is good.

17

THE SWEAT LODGE

The sweat lodge is one of the most important Indian practices. It is used to purify your mind and body. It is conducted before and after all other ceremonies.

All the elements that are found in our Mother Earth are present.

The fire that heats the stones represents the powers of the Creation and the sun.

The rocks represent our Mother Earth.

The water represents the changes of our lives.

The air represents the breath of our Mother Earth.

If you are invited to participate in a sweat lodge ceremony, ask your parents for permission to attend. It is important that the person conducting the sweat is qualified.

It is good.

18

THE VISION QUEST

When you are becoming an adult, you can go out to an isolated place to ask for a vision. This is called a vision quest.

This search for a vision means that you are in need of direction in your life. The Creation will show you the way. It can come from many places in nature or even from a dream.

Take a bedroll, your sage offerings pouch, strips of cloth in the colors of the four directions, and water. Place the colors of the directions about 15 steps apart. Place yourself in the center. Stay until you are satisfied within yourself that your answer has come.

Take an adult with you so that there is always someone nearby to attend to any of your needs and to conduct each sunrise ceremony.

It is good.

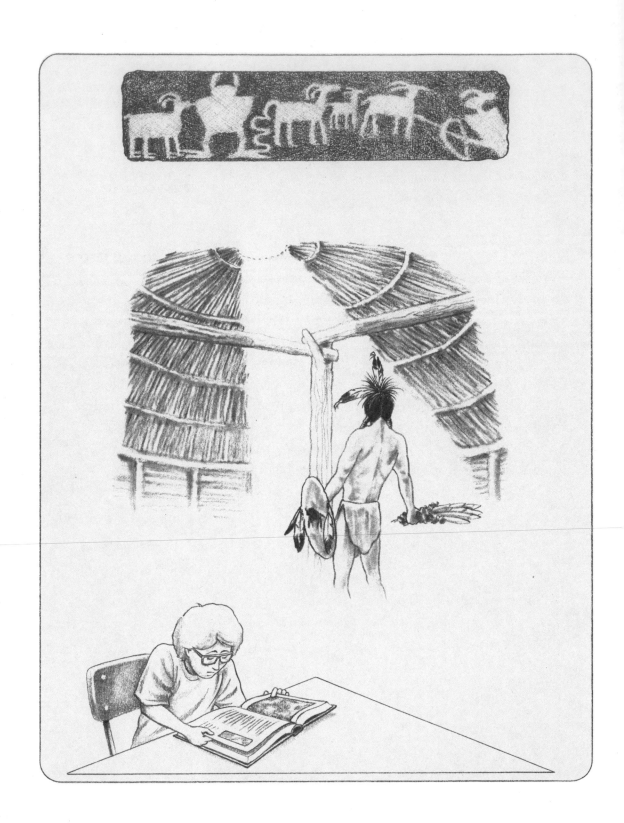

19

THE SUNDANCE

The Sundance is one of the most important ceremonies of many tribes. It was misnamed by non-Indians who thought it was about worshiping the sun. The true name is the Offering Lodge.

Those people who participate are giving themselves up to the Creation by fasting, without food and water, for up to seven days. Their purpose is to bring a good life for the people, their families, themselves, and for all living things, our relatives.

You can attend a Sundance at many places in America during the summer.

It is good.

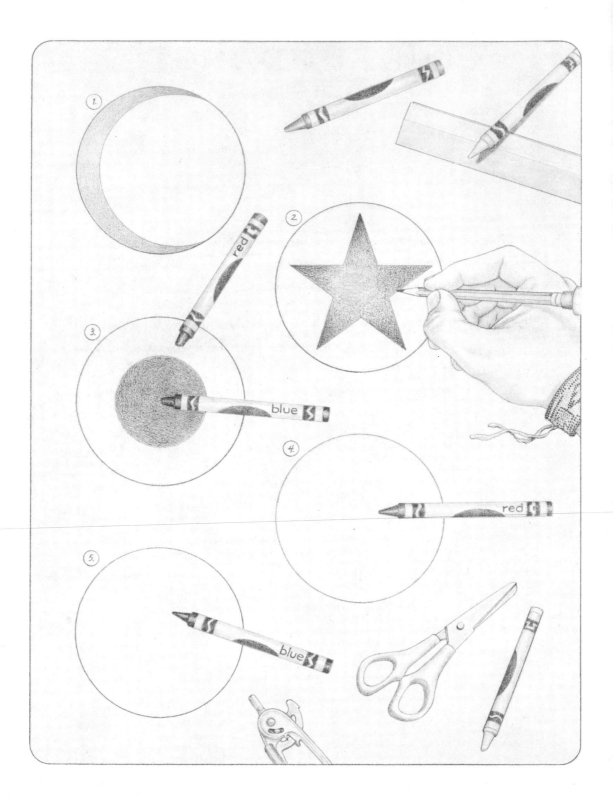

20

MEDICINE WHEELS

Medicine wheels are artistic expressions of the important things in our lives. You can make these medicine wheels from construction paper or cardboard and crayons or paints. Look at your medicine wheels every day and remember what each stands for.

①
The night sun or crescent moon. It
represents a person and everything that lives and dies.

②
The sacred morning star, which stands
between the darkness and the light.
It represents knowledge.

③
The sun; it represents the power to grow.
Our grandfather, which represents
all living things in the universe.

④
Our Mother Earth and all of her life:
all the two-leggeds, four-leggeds, the ones who fly,
the ones who swim, and the ones who
slither in the grasses.

⑤
The heavens and all our relatives,
all living things in the universe.

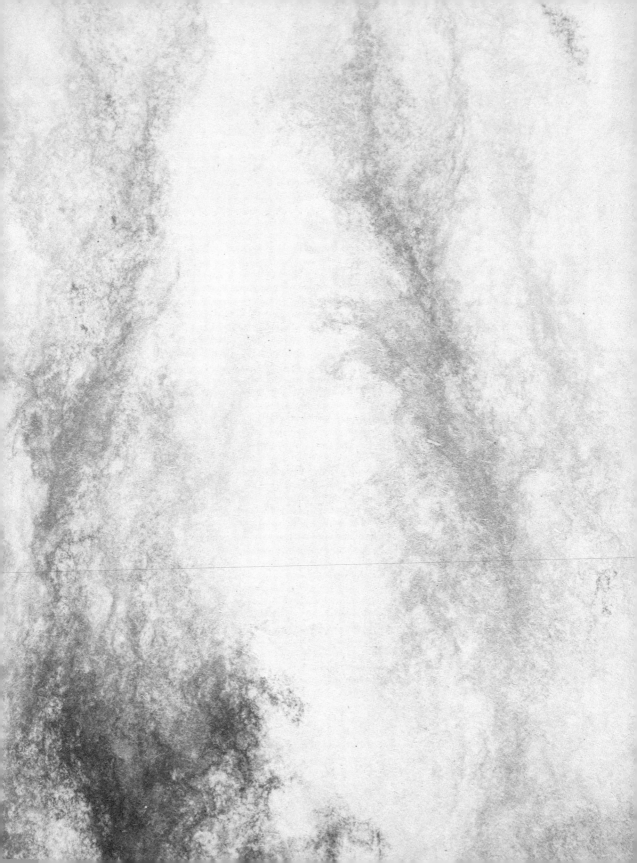

FOR MORE INFORMATION

To learn more about the Indian way of life and our environment, read:

Indian America by Eagle/Walking Turtle (Santa Fe, N.M.: John Muir Publications, 1989).

Keepers of the Fire by Eagle/Walking Turtle (Santa Fe, N.M.: Bear and Co., 1987).

The Sacred Pipe by Joseph Epes Brown (Norman: University of Oklahoma Press, 1953).

Touch the Earth by T. C. McLuhan (New York: Simon and Schuster, 1971).

When the Tree Flowered by John G. Neihardt (Lincoln: University of Nebraska Press, 1951).